VOLTE FACE

Dominique Hecq

Copyright 2024© Dominique Hecq

All rights reserved. This book or any portion thereof may not be reproduced or used in any manner whatsoever without the written permission of the publisher except for the use of brief quotations in a book review or scholarly journal.

 A catalogue record for this book is available from the National Library of Australia

Acknowledgement of Country

Liquid Amber Press is located in western Melbourne/ Naarm and we acknowledge the custodians and traditional owners of this unceded land, the Wurundjeri people of the Kulin Nation. We pay our respects to their Elders, poets and artists, past and present.

Cover image: René Magritte *'Les Amants', 1928* available through Wikimedia Commons

Cover design: David Hughes, DHC Creative

Published by Liquid Amber Press, 2024
PO Box 352, Seddon, Victoria 3011, Australia
www.liquidamberpress.com.au

ISBN 978-0-6457131-4-5

Hush! Caution! Echoland!
James Joyce

The regulating line is a guarantee against wilfulness.
Le Corbusier

Contents

Borges and I 1
Cursive 2
The Mechanics of her Brancusi Body 3
The Sound of Air 4
Travelogue Dalí 5
The Entombment 6
Anaphora 7
The Lord of Rats and Eke of Mice 9
Confession of a Bookworm 10
Five Bells 11
Archives of the Future 14
Exclusive 15
Cross-swell Heisenberg 16
Aseptic Perception 17
Twinklewinkalling 18
Ekphrastic Still 19
Epitaphios 20
Con Brio 21
Before the Moratorium 22
How It Is 23
Champagne Supernova, Taché 24
Bricks 25
Whimsical 26
Head Study 27
The Edge Land of Daydreams 29

Rrose Sélavy 30
Letter to a Bride to Be 31
Magritte's Gravestone 32
Dark Energy 33
A Haunting 34
Oblivion 35
Less Is a Bore 36
Telescopic 37
Magpies 38
The Language of Flowers 40
Endgame with No Ending 41
Volte Face 42
Bird Returning to its Nest 43
Dressed to the Nines 44
Blood Lines 45
Equinox 46
Liquid Desire 47
Evridiki 48
The Envoy 49
Child's Play 50
Homo Ludens 51
Anamnesis 52
Ξένος in the Sky 53
Either / Or 54
Rhythm 0 55
Inertia Carousel 56
Prosopagnosia 57

Aquatic 58
Εσπερινός 59
On the Heels of Fun 60
Fear of Birds 61
Swell 62
Wabi-Sabi 63
Flâneuses 64
Skin to Skin 65
Punctum 66
Fair Game 67
Reliquary 68
Schadenfreude 70
Gravity 71
Presence Follows Function 72
Breathless 73
Centaurs 74
The Doors 75

Contexts 77
Notes to Poems 78
Acknowledgements 85
About the Author 86

Borges and I

I sit by the opening of this labyrinthine library between a dark angel and his gossamer-clad acolyte. I point my boat out to sea, clutching memories of life and love, only to return to the shore. Its slippery pebbles, white and porous, soon grey with soot and red with rust: these bleed in trails of flickering flames. Borges's hair is on fire. He says poets have to remain with the concrete image. All language, I roll on, is abstract. Take the word rock: it's both more and less than an actual rock. He says all we could ever work with is the experience of the five senses. I say there are more than five senses. Thoughts, I say, are sensed and the movement of thought is perceptible; there are pre-verbal and pre-conceptual experiences. My skin is burning. Look, I snap, gesturing to the window: hail / flung at us // drops of water / trickling down the glass // sleet / refracting / baubles of light // hung in the sky's vault // rocks / fire-spiking // your mind's birded flight. And equally ready to fly, says Borges: words peck at your skull, their beak punctuating the long sentence of memory on the page of your mind. Time quietly leaves the scene: wind skimming over the surface of the sea like an infinity net, looping your breath to its rock face with a single monochromatic brushstroke. I extend my hand, try to touch his darkness. Don't cry for the moon, he says. I climb the rainbow into the night and reach for a web of stars, take a leap of faith and fall in a poem that reminds me of *Wuthering Heights*. I hear you calling. Feel the formlessness of the wind scratch my heart, unwinding its chambers and tributaries. I drink the moon dry.

Cursive

I hate Times Roman. Love Chancery Cursive. Love chance. Love gallivanting around the word. Chancery Cursive captures how the hand runs across the page. How letters get excited at the beginning of a piece. How they flourish in movement. Cursive lids the light, echoes mind-chambers and smells of honeysuckle. It gives body to sans-serif. Chancery Cursive takes off like writing in which the letters are joined and formed rapidly without lifting the nib of your pen, from the French *cursif*, from the Medieval Latin *cursivus*, from the Latin *cursus*, all run-running words. Even the past participle *currere*, meaning to run, from the Indo-European root **kers* that always reminds me what a curse a running hand is. Chancery Cursive is a marathon runner. It is tall and lean. It lives vertically, though it does embrace the wind in its course. It thrives on air, blood and water, seeds and nuts. Breeds dream-begotten strokes, forms, letters. *See how they run away* from Times Roman.

The Mechanics of her Brancusi Body

When I listen to a steel point on a copperplate, I inhale the moonflower yellow halo. Slip into hallucinogenic time. Images waft the way words glide by means of their sound alone. The Ferris wheel stops and you hang up in the night wind swinging in your little cage. Down below the woman in white is a frozen fountain. Her head balloons like a UFO against a sky of bat velocity. She holds her lunar hands in her lap. Watches out for light with her eyes closed. She's dead cells, cuticles, nails and ribbons of hair. She wants nothing from you. Cares nothing for you. I can see the severed stent in her heart. She's cold promise and futility. She's an overflow of severity. The mechanics of her Brancusi body propel her to the edge of *herternity*.

The Sound of Air

After Jean-Michel Folon

Moist as withheld rain, the haze is audible time. Lightning cuts into its soft belly. Tungsten numina in the near possible. No thunder.

Imagine a sphinx asking for silence. Eyes full stops. Mouth a line approaching the horizon past the Monet pond with blossoms of steel. How deep roots delve.

Tadpoles suck at my skull. Time's machine is intimately welded to my brain, or my brain to the machine. It identifies patterns as my hand moves across the page: serial structures, diversions, collages, quotations, allusions. Resistance to metaphor. Echolalia of autistic speech. Illogic. I am time itself, tending to what is no longer possible by subtraction when each and every detail is cut down to its essence. Object with no object. Uncroaking word presentation.

Travelogue Dalí

A procession of words legible as the horizon would be at a withheld point, withheld time: a washed out itinerary inside a seagull's gullet. Once a mermaid cavorting with Botticelli's Venus, you are now a mere pinprick principle vying with toxins, paperclips, peanuts, cigarette buts, skeins of silk, stirrups, socks, glyphs, icicles, exoskeletons, nails, cuneiforms, marbles and jellyfish. You grit your teeth. Select a monocle. Meticulously reconstruct the contortionist's honeymoon: wedding ring, lobster, credit card, hourglass, steel mesh, Bible, harp, condom, cross, knife, eyeball, scarf, Botox, blubber, Xanax, a print of Millet's *Angelus* and an alternative historical fiction set in Nazified France titled *The Grand Alliance*. You invoke the spirit of the praying mantis. A scenario begins to emerge. You reconnect with the pin part of your existential principle. Spellbound and tele-exiled, you fly from Melbourne to Nice where two thousand bloods run, filtering fables from far ago. Where all is dark shaken, veil over mass exodus. Where corpuscular clouds twine the sky and bells, every minute unhinged, toll for a soul. 'Tis done. You autograph your script. Unrushed, the millennial eagle soars in the pixelated dusk. God haemorrhages. You recede into cerise smoke.

The Entombment

In the sky-blubbering sea stands entombed a dead alive elephant with sawn tusks under a dome of azure ice. The elephant looks through me with pecked at lapis lazuli eyes. Its accusatory stare reaches not only beyond the sea but also beyond the horizon that bleeds into violet stars strewn on the crust of the earth. This could be a still from a Disney cartoon. A photograph from *Fantasia after the Apocalypse*. A hologram portending impending doom. I want to coax out the blue. But it would take days to knead and press and squeeze a dough of powdered lapis, wax, resin and linseed oil. Besides, the water is frozen and I have no wood ash. I'm Queen Boadicea dunked in woad cobalt oxide wailing for a child I never had. I'm a stone Buddha facing Ganesh. I'm Kubla Kahn turning Midnight Blue. I'm a petrified bird of paradise shooting through the Anthropocene. The elephant charges. Waves crash. I'm the Mount Lebanon Blue butterfly smashed to smithereens. I'm dancing matter that does not matter. I'm ultramarine. Utter darkness. I'm a mind unminding itself. Entombing itself. I'm *Ash in this sunless sea sinking in tumult to a lifeless ocean*. I'm molecules of oxygen and hydrogen. I'm particles of dust in frozen H_2O. In this inky *pleasure dome with caves of ice*. I'm nameless.

Anaphora

The day without ceremony begins with blackbirds. Bells unhinged. Silence is an air bubble breaking. I move amid feathers beneath unbuttoned eyes. Light. Unmusical yet rhythmical sounds echo in the room. Let's call her Voyce, face closed, she touches the fugue of language. Silence is an air bubble breaking, I say. A quizzical expression beclouds her face. Laughter bursts in her breath. I touch the sky. Phonemes cut the air. Images, words, letters cascade. Tropisms rustle inside. Voyce and I, one and the other conjoined in the obsolete art of conversing. All is a wave of sound. Tide of noise. Unmusical yet rhythmical. A horn blast. Funny how the world seeps through the conversation. Cracks meaning—sorry, that's not what I meant at all. Images, words, letters cascade. Litter the floor (the forward movement of speech is associative rhythm, connection, disconnection, repetition, disconnection, disrupted flux *tending-not-tending-to-hemiola*). Tropisms rustle inside. Voyce and I, one and the other conjoined in this disappearing life. We trail off into silence. I can be played on any instrument I, or Voyce, then says, *Shh Shh Shh*. Did you hear?

Hum. High and eerie keening. Voyce is not a person of many words. Her face closed, she touches the fugue of language before language. A fractal tune floats through the air. I gesture towards the piano. Puffing exhalations, chiming, puffing exhalations. Voyce sits down at the instrument. Rip tide of sound. I am speechless—one AND two AND three AND four AND five AND six AND… Her hands move so swiftly and fluidly on the keyboard of language before the fugue of language it's hypnotic. Black birds white birds black fish white fish black frogs white frogs. And winding up the performance one AND two AND three AND four AND five AND six AND seven AND Voyce finishes with a parodic flourish. Wow! We glide inwards towards the very centre of Escher's *Verbum*.

The Lord of Rats and Eke of Mice

The room is choked with chairs so worn grey motes rise from the seat covers, like mushrooms out of their mycelium. One by one, the chairs fill up. Kids sit on the floor, perch on armrests or hang from chandeliers. A rat with a clipboard takes down names. A white wolf pads through the door, brushes past heavy violet velour curtains, swivels dramatically on its paws, *moves upward*, as if *working out the beast*, and faces us. A vulture flies through the window, settles on the table, slouches slightly and surveys the mountains of eyeballs, blue beards, black teeth, torn fingernails, the fields of tiny rhinoceros horns and horse hooves and lion manes, the rivers of miracled moths and caterpillars and earwigs. A meerkat with a monocle pushes the vulture forward. Nods in the direction of a sphinx with eyes aglow. The floorboards shake. An eke of mice. We hold our inky scalpels aloft. Eat.

Confession of a Bookworm

The book is in a cardboard cover marked Fragile. I tenderly lift the volume out of its dogeared case. Scraps of leather binding and confettied paper fall on the floor in a cloud of organic matter. I wish I were an alchemist, botanist or physician, but my eyes naturally turn to calligraphy and flashes of colour. I kneel down. Sneeze. Finger the powder when out of the blue the Abbé Raynal storms into the library and screams: *MALHEUREUSE*! My fingers are red and as I try to rub the colour off the palms of my hands grow red. *MALHEUREUSE*! *Dactylopius coccus* holds the secret of cochineal. You will be tried for treason to the sound of thundering Spanish cannons and French trumpets. You will receive angry salutes from twenty-four pounders. And you will burn among phials and flasks and cases of books.

Five Bells

i.

An inverted slice of sky falls into *waves with diamond quills*. In the fiction room, the depth of night disgorges its obscurity, and the cold that numbs gradually lays its acid tongue on the back of my neck. The rhythm of the swell rhymes with my pulse. Heart beating in shadow, I lean into the dark. Energy all around laps at my ears. First star. Ebullience. My body soars inwardly. Out of control. Overflow of limits. Slows. My hand holds back the bleeding moon. Hovers over phantoms. Abolishes perspective. The uncanny feeling that the hand is writing, tracking the emergence of matter from before words. I listen for the sound of fish gills whispering on the shivering breeze. Rush of breath. Dull anguish, ready to drown desire. Quiver. Scuff of letters. Gravity in ink. Chrysalis calligraphy.

ii.

Down at the curving wharf the ferry, yellow and green and wooden, chugs away to the north. Some say you had no ticket but pockets full of grog. Heaving rain, bursts like violent sobs. Disgorgement. Waves clamour. Reflections from the deep. A wind that doesn't dry; it's thirsty. Rattles invisible sails. An intoxication of possibilities. Time deep enough to sink in ships over the horizon. Five bells ringing from a vessel at its moorings. No witness to the engulfment of the body clad in your tattered raincoat. Clatter of glass bottles. Night drinks all but you are still thirsty. The skyline flattens. The bed of an eager sea claims you like a mother.

Gathers you in a swell of stars. The harbour quivers with foam. Sydney gorged with water. You, mouthless, flesh, fishy silt. Your legend, tongue-tied beat of time.

Ariadne Dreams of a New Relativity

Pitch black. No water. The monster's breath is cold and smells of carrion. Always in debt, once bankrupted, arrested and imprisoned, now he's in hiding. Though he roars and curses and says the universe is but a huge expletive I'm not scared (been there before). *Shh. Shh. Shh.* Think of the metaphysical implications of black holes, dark matter, the big bang and string theory. We could expand the Labyrinth with a slew of metaphors. Slay all the fake gods of Logos, purge their purgatories, destroy Limbo and generate new galaxies where you could hear the light. Touch God's parched skin. Grind Time's bristles. Wring Death's neck. Galaxies where shooting stars would surge and rush, swell and fall. Now, give me a rope. Let's sing to the glory of the Minotaur.

Archives of the Future

After Oscar Dominguez

Stench of the born-again wild beast slouching towards infinity. The horizon spouts clouds. Your typewriter and its neuron words settle on time's cleft. Craters rise to the skies, witnesses to history's expunged signs.

In the beginning you imagined cold air on skin, white gloves, pencil, paper. Enlisted words undercutting representation's factual value. But people are ever puppets on strings held by ungloved hands. They leap out of musty pages, return you to *arkhē*'s suffixal form, *arkheion*. Skip the record of a lifetime's metaphors, wielding words from the paterfamilias' house, to unanimous chorus, to Law Court.

The body's storehouse gathers abjection's silt; it is the cave where defiance buried you alive—call it Thebes, Bedlam, Holloway, or Other. It is where duty and language never collide with memory on your sister's lips. Yet words are not bats to be released from caves. They are birds set free from cages to open the heart's secret chambers. Inviolate, they are open to revision, still. See how they spread their wings. How high they soar.

Exclusive

Sugar free? Not a problem, *monsieur*, says the waiter, a smile momentarily sweetening his sour face. We have an exclusive *carte* of sugar free desserts. *Les oeufs à la neige*, of course, from our own free range silkie hens, are quite succulent. The egg whites are poached in simmering goat's milk and served on warm vanilla infused custard topped with dazzling dahlias. *Les cœurs à la crème* are divine but, naturally, more calorific. They are served with passionfruit coulis, *crème fraîche* and violets. *Le Paris Brest*, our chef's specialty is sculpted out of gluten free choux pastry, then filled with alcohol free Cognac infused *crème fraîche* and topped with dark sugar free Godiva chocolate, toasted almond flakes and a sprinkle of pure vanilla bean frost. It is served with crimson nasturtiums reclining on soft peaks of clouds made to the chef's secret meringue recipe. *Deep breath*. The almond *jalousie* is also sugar free; it is sweetened with organic raw blue agave—fairtrade certified. It is served with hot pink glams and zero alcohol Grand Marnier cream. Very popular are the mini cream horns baked until golden and crisp. They are filled with *crème fraîche* just before serving on a bed of snapdragons and violas—to die for. Last, but not least, we have *les poires exquises* poached in sugar free alcohol free sulphate free Sauterne imported from the Caves du Dauphin in Reims—the pears are fructose free. At that, the ecstatic waiter closes his eyes, upturns his face and whispers: they are calorie free.

Cross-swell Heisenberg

Sky shot with stars. A heartbeat. The water's edge is shrouded in fog. The sea is butterfly bones soaking in moon loom frizz. Crackling breeze. A whale cries out. You sit right on the edge of the cliff as if you are you are Shelley, hair floating algae, air shocked out of your lungs. A brinkness. About face. Whitecaps fume and flicker. Rollers gush. Break. Stones flip up on the shore. A cavernous ribbed ragged *Schaumkrone* leaf wave rises up to the white horse moon. Thunder. Flash of light. Rain. Dappled grey nightmare. The mare rears. Kicks. It's an emergency metaphor. A catachresis made flesh. Hailstones. A piano mannequin lolls in the tide. Washes up. Unshackles. Her face is a tidal luminescence. The waves run away from the storm. Pomegranates explode. Glass skittles along the coral reef-ish shoreline. Everything from green to the outer edges of violet catches on fire. Between us, flitting flies glitter. A song breaks. It's a cavalcade of giraffes: *Gravida*.

Aseptic Perception

I extinguish those go get eyes. Welcome a winged victory. I want to believe there is an absence of hate love in this pandemonium. This blue pestilence. This soaked paper aeroplane with a broken wing grounded for all eternity next to the angel of history. They macerate in octopus ink, the plane and the angel. Sombre tones seep through the monochromatic scheme only a maniac could have devised. A paranoiac godlet from IMAGING, says something spawned by *Les Chants de Maldoror*, a reverie that moves associatively and appositionally to cover and uncover the most extravagant images and proclamations of abjection. Say it! Declare imminent hostilities. Grill some brains with mashed sardines and anchovies. Char us, squashed as we are in this corset you call a room when we are meant to explore the limits of painting. Assassinate poetry. Resurrect prose. Only to describe, define and affirm the visible. Portray. No. Poetic physiology is not the physiology of living creatures, though minds unmind after blasted hearts. Nothing is *d'après nature*. Eat that nothing mixed with blitzed green chilli, coriander, lime juice, olive oil, absinth. See what I destroyed. Taste what I did mean.

Twinklewinkalling

Lilac and jasmine in the air. Indigo. Violet light of a grave-lit moon. Black motes swirl in iridescent blue. Whirl, twirl and settle on your name. Jay—from the Latin for Gaea. You always wanted to fly, but have been grounded a lifetime. God knows I tried to change the script. I look for all *twinklewinkalling* gone. A Rorschach is what you left. Cold blade lips. A palimpsest of bruises. Vacated are your emerald eyes. Winter is in your mouthless mouth. I imagine your dreams, realities, nightmares, suffocations. Once you told me in your waking life you flew. Despite the grounding. How you feared falling off bridges. It was vertigo and agoraphobia took your breath away. No angel wings here, though they say they are always blue. How many times can you die? I zero in on the white hole of the question mark. No breath. Your throat, cinereous grey, is lined with needles. A thimbleful of bluish light. A chrysalis. Cells twitch, uncurl, zizz out. Fizz beyond imaging, beyond the apocalypse of bloods and tissues, beyond the wildest imaginings. A noose dangles, lonely; motes whirl in the luminescence of day—a drama you staged in air and liquid desire for your solitary pleasure.

Ekphrastic Still

These walls are made of language as tough as granite. We built them together word by word, syllable by monosyllable, letter by letter. Scraped them clean of dreams after you'd spent all our love on the irreal real. I stole all the rhymes, assonances, alliterations, intervals, elisions and silences to get you back. But you spread *crépi* all over the concrete and I stuck little barbs and hooks in it as it dried. I swore to have these walls ruined. Even drew up plans. The first part of the scheme was the Poeisis Tower. It was designed for use without melting clocks. You packed it with biblical and medieval iconography. So, I splashed mortar all over. Stuck a sign on it saying FOR RESTORATION and ran away before succumbing to your murderous fantasies. A great loss to the history of craftsmanship, but a tribute to the unfinished story of *l'Amur*. I should have considered the possibility of a Real Staircase emulating Late Lacanian Baroque.

Epitaphios

The curtain has risen on the red stage. A little girl awaits my return. The seats are empty everywhere about her torn ribboned dress, waning and the mauled circumference of her face, a waning moon, already carries the echo of words hovering above murmurs. Here are the corridors. Here the machines. I catch my gaze on the other side of window panes because I know the silence where I am locked in. Vowels at the apex of disembodied voices announce the lostness of a near forgotten woman. The intermission consumed, my child remembers and I look for the trail of her violet dark. The whitened crepuscular arch I have become step by step covers pathways and at the fork, throws a dice. Ace, red viburnum tooting its horn in nocturnal trance. Passing through the pink light a flightless angel pronounces the apotheosis for tomorrow, cups his face and heads where the dead are born, gather the fire of the sky and dance where ashes scatter underneath. I taste the salt of shadows, feel their lumpy texture, thirst for coal. Muzzle bloated sounds. Listen. Hear one pop after the other. Simultaneity of cavernous spaces. Panegyric vengeance. There is only one obolus: the step on an inept trace. Already erased.

Con Brio

After Antonio Vivaldi, Venice 1678 - Vienna 1741

I want it alive. Hold my breath. Summon my instrument. The marvellous pharynx at the top and back of my throat throbs in my mind's eye. I see the constrictors, muscles of the soft palate and eustachian tubes that connect the top of my throat to the middle ear. I hear you say in my head *buccinator, mandible, orbicularis oris*. Taste the words. Swallow. Breathe in. Pull in my cheeks and lash out at Vivaldi's clamorous, insistent, racing strings: *Se lento encora IL FULMINE*. The air ignites. I am the Big Bang. The birth of the world. My own birth. Duplicitous Argippo's death. I come alive inside and outside the cascade that fills the stage. My voice booms. EX-plodes. OVER-flows. Drowns Vivaldi's strings. Drowns ARGH-ippo. Death to geminate faced Argippo whose love was many of its own kind. BOOM! KA-BOOM! Death to all cunning bastards! The pharynx at the top and back of my throat throbs. Constricts. Unties. The rage of all women roars in this single voice in the da capo: *SE LENTO ENCORA IL FULMINE*.

Viz. *Argippo, Dramma per Musica, Libretto da Domenico Lalli, Atto Primo.*

Before the Moratorium

It starts with a rattle. Not wooden, but silvery. It's not a song. Beautiful people spring from nowhere. They hover in a no wo/man's land between the earth and the sky. They head for the embankment, jiggling coins in the pockets of gossamer robes, presumably hoping to return from their Katabasis. They glide down three white marble steps and into the ebony pirogue. One single Obol, hollers Kharon, daggers in his eyes. The daggers cut open intricately embroidered purses. The ferryman hurls all the useless clickety coins in the black river, slick as oil. Out of time, and now space, the beautiful people are a van Eyck painting. Ten beautiful bodies dangle from the rafters Death makes with her legs; they arch their backs, contort, writhe, grimace. One hides under Death's phantom calf. Most squirm, wriggle and thrash about among beasts with yellow eyes and sharp teeth. There are dragons and snakes and panthers and rats, pumas and crows and hyenas. A beautiful woman goes by on a stretcher in the solid grip of two firemen clad in royal blue. She's propped up, almost sitting – serene, with grey hair, her face unlined. A blood-spattered blanket conceals her legs and half her torso. She crosses the square crowded with kids. Chants *If the children are happy they are communists*.

How It Is

It's the end of a summer day on the bus where a little girl, or is it a boy, rocks their Barbie doll and I, sitting figurine in decomposition, have no word to describe the light, the sky's absolute perfection and the wheels of the clouds going *round and round, round and round*. Just as one presumes that paradise exists, one assumes that reality exists. The reality of the clouds high above the mountain. The foothills and escarpments covered in trees and not at all bare as I would draw them were a child to ask me to *Plea-ease* draw me a mountain with a sheep atop. A light between sky and clouds and mountain. A Jurassic light. A flicks and dinosaurs kind of light. The diplodocus neck of the light with the sky its absolutely perfect skeleton. I don't want to know the first word I'll say when you leave. I want to live in real time with the summer you and the clouds going *round and round, round and round* and the wind going *swish* and *swish* in real light outside the bus.

Champagne Supernova, *Taché*

Starlight, annular. Self-luminous and thermonuclear coils in a nest. Shot silk. Alive taffeta. Scales, feathers, down, fur, skin. Pinkish brightening against the jet-black sky. Implosion. Compression. Explosion. Spicules. Your eyes, red-rimmed, hurt with gaseous light unlighting. Spectroscopic pulsation of pinks and reds. Slow whirl of carmine, vermillion, *giroflée*, red lead, scarlet pink, fuchsia, baby pink, rust-speckled traces of brain matter. Swirling cloud of hydrogen, helium, carbon, neon, oxygen, silicon. You plunge into your own dismembering body. Rise up to the surface. Cool down. Plunge again, *inwardoutward*. Cicadas scurry through your *bodymindsoul*, carnation-darnation chills. You breathe in tantric fashion when what you need is an antipyretic, analgesic, emetic. *Pfffff...* Fast slow entropy. Hundreds of billions of years in three little seconds, snuffed. Three caskets in stellar atmosphere. No, *Herr Doktor*, this is no hallucination. *This is the* real real. Life leaches away from you. Tubular bells. Church quiet. A whiff of incense and black sun. *The world's still spinning round, we don't know why... Gegenschein*. Light curve. Crepuscular rays. Green flash. Twinkle. You sail ahead of *timenotime* into the dark bubbling out of gravitas. Radiate your own heat. Blow apart in a brilliant anti-anthropic stellar body dispersing on the other side of the eclipsing pillars of creation, purple lake, ultra-deep charcoal shades. The Dead Sea *Asphaltum*. Stardust, afloat.

Bricks

Eclipse. The girl woman dances, ghetto blaster full boom. Opens her eyes as the door bashes open. Damn, she says inside her head, caught off-guard. He presses STOP. Takes the cassette-player. Pig music, says Father, all scorn. Confiscated. One month. Shrug (the girl woman recalls He said the same about *The Rite of Spring*). Skating on thin ice, girl. Two months. Glare. The girl woman swims. Steep channels branching off into fishways enable fish to swim upriver. But she's only a fishlet holding tears back. She smells the pigsty: reek of shit and putrefaction. She summons an igloo. Loves domes: walls exert equal thrust in all directions. She is the tension queen block. Ice window. The tunnel joining her living quarters with the storm igloo. She keeps an eye on the entrance and air hole, *presentpastfuture*. The gone ghetto blaster hums. Weep hole, cramp, flush. Masonry is memory, music, imagining. For two months, the girl woman thinks of the break in *The Wall* that holds her together. She fashions bats and closers she never dreamed might lead to an exit. Chase on course, she knows light lurks in flesh brick Pink of Floyd.

Whimsical

We are polishing off our *Once and Well* chardy under a silver wattle bursting forth in millions of golden blossoms at Hanging Rock when we notice a track leading into the forest. We follow it past clumps of stringy bark and peppermint gums as it winds beside the river dappled with late winter light. Warm wind gusts from up the gully. Thin stalks of grass billow like your bald man's comb-over. We marvel at the large multi-branched trees with smooth white bark shedding in curling ribbons, dense spreading crowns of long narrow leaves, rough barked trunks underneath. You joke that manna gums are notorious for dropping large limbs. Yes, often fatal, I riposte. We push on, stamping our feet on the leaf-littered dry, not noticing the clouds of gnats hovering in the air, the tiny swooping ravens. There is a chill in the air. We stumble on an old hollow tree quartering an army of gnomes, some bearded, some bald, but mostly clean-shaven as if ready for a hard day's work. *Hey ho. Hey ho.* Carved on the hollow's lip is a sign: GNOME SWEET GNOME. We chuckle. Take a closer look at the little fellows. So sweet, you say, in a surreal way. I dunno; they look… I say, trailing on a word's shadow — sinister. Nah, it's a lovely whimsical thing. A snort. I'm an old friend, says the wind, softly. Then screams: KILL THEM!

Head Study

Now that it's done, I pore over the work. It looks like a radiography of your head in profile. Your mouth is neither open nor closed; lips faintly stretched in a grimace; you ate your smile.

… anger makes one clench one's teeth, terror and atrocious suffering make the mouth the organ of tearing cries …

I hear Adrian Leverkühn's diabolical laughter and it doesn't want to fade. Recall that somewhere Julia links laughter to cries, for both are *evaporation of meaning and the only possibility of communication*. Antonin would have screamed. Both are speechless—mere spasms of the body. The inarticulacy of overflowing emotion.

I love the monocle you wear in death. You look as though you went blind in art's headlights. How Joycean!

I gave you sanitised memories and a brain tumour named after *Le Lac Majeur*. If I rotate the work, you are an axolotl burdened with signs that come alive. Could have spawned snakes wreathing, Gorgon-like. But it was music I was after.

Chance marks thrown, scrubbed, sponged to trap the real real. Break the spell.

In this last letter from you, the carpet of your mind oozes black blood because fear makes the heart burn black.

And squirting out a sharp death-gush of blood / It strikes me with dark drizzle of murderous dew.

You slip out of sight.

The Edge Land of Daydreams

I've never counted the bones in my hand, but I have an extra finger shaped like a honey eater's beak—an esoteric bit of fleshed out bone that blocks all light except the liquid bandwidth emitted by ionised hydrogen in burning honey that reveals the cloying structures of gas corralled by magnetic fields and birds of paradise. My extra finger enables me to feel the inside of blackwood buds. Taste the nectar of their nebulae-filled umbraphile flowers. Smell the heat of what will be called this year's hydrogen alpha bee bushfire. See the next total eclipse of the sun at Exmouth. Capture the cosmic inferno that will be known in one thousand and one nights. The mother of utter silence buoyant with premonitions.

Unwrite the I from the poem.

Mid-walk, the skies open. Rain pours. Yellow water rises, swirling about, soon gushing out of the broken creek's banks, carving furrows among grass, reeds, bushes and trees. The dog takes the lead and pins us to the bridge. Murky calm where the path tilts and narrows. Here, the water curves and swerves in its owns bed, pulls at silt. The current pushes it out unseen, against the sunken stepping stones. Here, the water swirls, froths, falls and rushes towards the edgeland of daydreams. Towards the unregulating of the line.

Rrose Sélavy

C'est moi, says Marcel Duchamp, my cross-dressed body trans-figured into readymade in furs—almost *femme fatale*, lipsticked and bejewelled, intent on luring Man Ray and André Breton like some erotic algorithm, uncanny signature pointing to the gap between ego and alter, retinal and anti. Such art—or is she merely oxymoronic, already fetishized?

Rrose's own preference, never for binary programs, nudges up through one hundred years of seeming oblivion in the dim lights of libraries, studios, art catalogues.

How sharp the eyes in the averted gaze says an angel with horns called René Magritte, thus signing Rrose's enucleation with the stroke of an apocryphal phrase.

Letter to a Bride to Be

Thank you for sharing with me the newest (yet quite retro) issue of *Vogue Bridal Patterns*. I love that off-white shot silk you brought back from your travels and think it would suit your complexion perfectly. It looks much better than the Nora white organza. It's also a tribute to your integrity and I hope I'm not reading too much into your choice of colour. But before you start making the dress, I urge you to indulge in a little intertextual journey around your maiden room, if I may say so, for I'm not sure you know on what *galère* you are embarking. Mark my words. I don't mean *gondola*, or anything romantic, but *galley*, a low, flat ship with one or more sails (glad you opted for a visor instead of a veil) and up to three banks of oars worked by slaves. First, as an artist, you must re-read Tennyson's 'The Lady of Shalott' against the grain. Then turn to Elizabeth Bishop's 'The Gentleman of Shalott' and Jessica Anderson's *Tirra Lirra by the River*. I studied both in year twelve (wish I'd paid more attention). Finally, and this may surprise you, especially coming from me, read Henrik Ibsen's *A Doll's House*, a work your father drew on to devise our home. Deep down, I now think Ibsen understood the difference between need and desire; desire and love; love and lust. Your father would disagree, of course, but I would maintain that Ibsen was really a proto-feminist writer. *Wink*. One last thing: beware of identifications. With two (anti)heroines bearing your Christian name, you wouldn't want to become unduly hystericised.

Magritte's Gravestone

draws on the *faculty which perceives at once, quite without resort to philosophic methods, the intimate and secret connections between things, correspondences and analogies* from Baudelaire to Lautréamont to Breton to Magritte, who *used to provoke ... shock by causing the encounter of unrelated objects.* It would have to be called *Elective Affinities*, after a novel by Goethe. So, just as an image results from preliminary *investigations and accidental encounters*—say a bicycle & a cigar or a cigar & a fish (with smoke curling and swirling up) at the *intersection* of a paradoxical *synthesis of antithetical concepts* or *interpenetrating images*, the poem is *tacitly comprised of objects that remain to be found.* Think of 'The Seducer' (1950), where *the sea takes the form of a ship,* or authorised 'Plagiarism' (1960), where *a bouquet on a table has been replaced by the landscape outside. In this painting the antithetical concepts 'inside' and 'outside' (or 'here' and 'there') have been synthesized in a single image, but they are also still understood as two images by the mind* as are three perfect eggs in a nest.

This sentence waits to migrate past the confines of the page. It's moonstruck. Watch its metamorphosis.

Ceci n'est pas une pipe: we are made of letters. Look how they liquefy in the inkpot.

Dark Energy

A thwack. You sink into yourself. An explosion of elementary particles. You are a supernova shooting through air and stars. A baryonic ball of bleeding energy scattering matter in the void. Your heart beats out of place like wind gusting on a high plain. Pulse hovers on a knife edge. You wriggle out of your body. Crawl through gaseous clouds to a rocky alcove they call emergency. Climb the lookout they call a chair. Fall into antigravity. Whizz through a constellation of voices eying your soul from the back of beyond. Black out in a heaving orange cloud where spider flowers rustle the air. When you come to Nurse Vera Aguilar she tells you not to touch your stitches or it will scar. You take your eyes off her badge. Stare at her face as though through a telescope. This is what a black hole looks like in a spark chamber.

A Haunting

Wading into fallen stars that stream towards the mouth of forgetting as surely as Heinrich von Kleist's self-appointed gun, you catch a glimpse of my mask, Orpheus. It is red like a child's first blood. It smells of wattle, musk and frangipani. It sounds like mirrors smashing shadows though the moon is high and full of Dürer's kinetic hues. As the curtain of the archive of the world of the living lifts, your anamorphic skull comes into view. In that hypnagogic instant I catch a glimpse of the heart from which I'll die: it is surrounded by swans taking on the hour's changing colours. I feel fluff, plumes, feathers, quills, barbs, spines, spikes. I think of Dalí's aphasic metaphors. Hear Kandinsky's asphyxiated screams. Wait for your otherworldly cry. It is like crystal shattering one thousand and one nights before the invention of the word plumage and it does not end. D minor. *Decrescendo.*

Oblivion

The bearded puppet with the strings sliced looks into your cranial cavity. Relax, he says. *The indifferent memories of childhood owe their existence to a process of displacement: they are substitutes in reproduction, for other impressions which are really significant.*

The puppet takes out his slide rule, calculates the space between now and then. The space between what happened and the stories we tell. The puppet considers your incredulity. Rolls his huge wooden eyes at you: *I started from the striking fact that a person's earliest childhood memories seem frequently to have preserved what is indifferent and unimportant, whereas... no trace is found in an adult's memory of impressions dating from that time which are important.*

You want to know what's wrong with your archival ability. The puppet's nose grows as long as the slide rule: There is nothing wrong with your, err—brain.

Less Is a Bore

The house, a Multiplex hologram, stands against the wind, facing the fallen world at Chestnut Hill, Philadelphia. The façade evokes a child's picture of a Georgian mansion: arch above the doorway, lintel coursing through it, gable recalling a classical pediment. It is split at the apex, suggesting the brokenness of time and home. The crossed-out window to your left is a pastiche of 'The Kiss,' It celebrates architecture as art, opening into new realms of creation. The strip windows at your right express the man-child's desire to move out. The house is like a poem. It conjures up the human need for stimulation, surprise, change. Its vocabulary is eclectic, inventive. Inside there are no curtains, no blinds blocking out the world. The studio, where some of this world swings by for a chat, a drink, a laugh, I call contingent. Here, among yuccas, orchids, bonsais and African violets, I mess with words, lines, shapes, structures, images, rhythms, textures. This is where poems, drawings, paintings, sculptures, maquettes and garments evolve, intertwining time and space under the piercing gaze of Antonin Artaud.

Telescopic

A knock at the door. How could that be at a time of confinement? Normally you would peek through the curtains but now that all glass has been replaced by tightly fitting stainless-steel windows, you're caught at your own game, Professor. *Knock. Knock. Knock.* A glance at the computer screen. You should be worried, you know. For decades you've been knocking at the door of civil and military space agencies, trying to get access to sounding rockets and satellites because in your eyes space has theoretical as well as technical advantages such as the absence of gravity and a low level of thermal perturbations. Feel how cold the house is. How it begins to rock. And look: your telescope's marching across the room now, its big eye fastened on you.

Magpies

A whiff of butter, caramel, French fries and booze in the air that swells in the city's cooing clamour. Voiceless, you follow your feet. Up and up they climb the bumpy cobbled streets toward the medieval castle's remains. All around, the walls of the old town radiate heat. Up they walk you, your feet, to the tipping point of the landscape. They take you to Villa Noailles. Closing time. You sit down on a garden bench. Your parched skin soaks in stray droplets of water from the sprinklers. You wonder what time they close the gate. Notice the height of the iron fence.

She arrives the way birds do. Soundlessly. Fleetingly. Drinking the air. Irony in her gaze. She perches next to you. Unties your tongue: Bird, you say, don't mind me I'm only gathering fragments of living.

The bird woman laughs. Asks if you've been to the salt marshes on the Giens peninsula. Says she loves waterbirds. That you should go to Porquerolles; walk the rocky trails and snorkel in the *criques* for they are full of underwater shipwrecks. This would suit you, who inhabit no space, but time's broken line.

Vous n'êtes pas très loquace, says the bird in this strange tongue full of understatements, reiterations, reproaches, this plu-perfect tongue that once allowed you to renounce what might have been.

Words shot with odours of butter and caramel, echoes, sensations. Melting moments. And now this bird woman with a tongue as sharp as a blade who converses silently with magpies in the brokenness of time. Hyères, betwen dog and wolf. Anything could happen.

The Language of Flowers

We file to the *Maison Communale*. Climb the rickety stairs. Enter the *Chambre des Mariages*. The *proches* congregate around *madame le maire*: *Prenez place*. All sit down. I march to the far back of the room. Stand. The mayor's speech is an antiquated list of spousal duties with doors between words. Napoleon smirks.

I want to slap off my niece's blooming mask. Distract myself with her bouquet of lilies dangling against the virginal satin of her dress. Like all plants, flowers belong to a family. In the binomial nomenclature of Linnaeus, that of genus and specific name: splendid sexual system and lexicon of parts. The ex-wife glides into the room, her velvet suit, undulating algae. From the Latin *alliga*, meaning to bind, to entwine, to bandage, to fetter or fasten; but also to hold fast, hinder, detain, or to oblige, to lay under obligation. *Vive la divorcée!* I wonder if she kept his name, the groom's first mate. Everyone speaks of her sweetness. I smell agarwood and hemlock; its bitter aphrodisiac odour.

Endgame with No Ending

You too, once thought you were on top of your game. After the Titans of the University were defeated, you shared a hot desk on Mount Olympus with astronomists and astrophysicists who, unlike you, conducted their collaborative research behind the closed doors of their laboratories. Every third Friday of the month you would meet at the Pantheon, the space where all the vigorous discussions among the scientists and chief administrators took place. Then one fateful morning you packed your meagre pile of books and moved to the foot of Mount Parnassus (the handful of linguists and historians and philosophers had long disappeared). Having embraced the principle of heterogeneity inscribed within the very ethos of Parnassus, you devoted yourself to a theatre of dreams, visions, mirrors, smoke-screens and metaphors where images replace imitations that generate specular emotional responses in a constant act of deconstruction to reveal the core of an encounter of self with other. Now you exhume your life on the sTREEt OF croCODilES. Cymbals!

Volte Face

It's day one and there is no way out. I dash out the door. Follow her through streets sizzling in noon sun. Her back is burnt like ox hide. Her hair is glowing ruby. Though she remains an indistinct figure with a limp I name her Philomena. I follow her through the hotel gate. Revolving door. Entrance lobby. Two pairs of glassy eyes. Let them call the police. Room 33. She goes through. I close the door. She turns around. My blood chills. Did she recognise me? I hide behind my phone. Take a picture. Flee. Cops with blue beards at the gate. I tear through. This is a noir gone awry. An experiment in how to lead an investigation. It works by means on figuration and indirection. Out of breath, I stop in my tracks. Lost. I take out the phone from my pocket. In the photo her features are indistinct. Her steel eyes cut through the screen. The air bristles. Mother! Who sent you? I freeze. Her hair comes alive with snakes.

Bird Returning to its Nest

After Georges Braque

O stands before the pond. Through sheets of mist, she sees something fluttering on the opposite bank: a man, spinning. His charcoal robes whirl and whirl in a sky heavy with storm. His hair whips into his eyes. His knuckles, saturnine as he clenches his fists and spins faster and faster. O reaches for him. Mouths unspoken words. He stops. Looks at her. Fever is a motion sensor. Ping! Sting of sunlight through duckweed clouds. Rain pours in thick ropes. They fall up or down. A pigeon coos feebly, as encaged. The bird flies across. Wings through the bottom of the pond, its frayed feathers catch mommia night, twice burnt sienna and blood rust. Cuttlefish shrink to a Stockhausen phrase. The bird folds dovely into jaundiced buff.

Tang of incense and myrrh. Bells hush. *Knowing what to do by the tug of the brush,* O joins the cortege of snuffed out candles and mouthless pallbearers towards her nest, empty as a mathematical abstraction.

Dressed to the Nines

Ø takes the lift up to the ninth floor. She opens the gate. Sees that the door was ajar. Knocks. No answer. She pushes the door open, softly. The room is darker than an alley from the Middle Ages but a light coming from the bathroom casts a triangular shape on the teal carpet, making it look like the Mediterranean on an overcast day. Ø ambles to the bathroom. An octopus fills the toilet bowl. Its head is wreathed in dreadlocks writhing like snakes. Lipstick is smeared around its beak. One tentacle is cut off and it dangles like Marat's arm in Jacques-Louis David's famous painting. The knife is still attached to the appendage stuck to the shower recess. The octopus is so thin it would be floating had it not been weighed down by costume jewellery. Amid the fake pearls and diamonds is a huge pendant of the kind some wear with a lock of hair curled inside. Ø opens it. Sees her own withered face in faded sepia.

Blood Lines

After René Magritte

That night we drank black blood / disregarding Homer's warning / in Book XI of *The Odyssey* // the inner river's / propensity / to overflow and petrify / despite the will to forget // two wars coursing through our veins / the three caskets of our blood lines / four languages caught in static // might we awake, blotched browed, in the fourth / dimension, with half a face caught in a murder of silhouettes / and life's desiccated leaf curdled blood light?

Equinox

Sun, high. Folds of foliage whoosh up the clouds and fall. Whoosh and fall. Light and shadow kaleidoscope. Your feet stomp along the Merri Creek track. You peer into people's backyards and driveways. Here they advertise an Australian orgy at nightfall. BE THERE OR BE SQUARE. You trip. Slip. Twist. Scurry downstream through the wallaby grass. Slow down as you approach the road. Stop. A black stork. Roar of a Jeep. There's a toddler perched on a bumper seat next to the driver. No seatbelts. Roar. Scream of tyres. Dust explodes in gloaming sun straw. Bells ring. A mastiff barks at you. Dribbles. You glare. Push on. A woman's luminescent face zooms towards you. Look, she says, showing off the scythe sketched on her forearm, I'm going to have it inked. Your heart skips a beat. Nice, you say. Push on. Climb the path towards the overpass. A teenager, hands black and blue, strums his untuned guitar, head lolling. You drop a coin in the ceramic toad's open mouth. He upturns his pockmarked face. Looks at you, dazed. Cyclists whizz past. You round the corner indolently, curating the anodyne story of your life. Light and shadow kaleidoscope. *Whoosh.* Your head explodes on the kerb.

Liquid Desire

From the sea, an odour of tumescence. On the shore, turmeric turbulence. Tympani usurp overtones of thunder. Voracious mouths chuck upscale notes. Strident vapours. Magenta mayhem. A finger pressed on blackberry lips you taste kelp. Hanker after air. Suck in a school of fish. Gobble a lobster, telephone, melting watch, moustache, violin, a whole giraffe. Skulls and seahorses. Bubbling masses of nipples. The bleeding world and the tree of life. You are Gala and Elsa, Daphne and Apollo, Tristan and Isolde. You weigh down dyskinesia. Kneel before Fa Luca's *De Divina Proportione*. Take off through a chorus of seagulls like a hyperbole. Quixotic desire leaks into lines of flight. You are the Angel of Portlligat. The Madonna of the Aquamarine. Galatea of the spheres. Gold liquor Ophelia atomised.

Evridiki

You were born in autumn and so, naturally, hate spring. A butcher bird sings your metamorphic body. Cloying scent of blackwood showering pollen. Air licked with gold where the buzzing of bees deepens. The sudden opacity of it all. You run. Run away. Away from the visible and from the invisible. With the pollen clinging to your skin, the sun striking and the darkness beneath your feet settling on gravel. You are a living phobia. A fear of no consequence. Yet as aeons pass in one beat of your beating heart, you hear the rustle under the tree limbs. Taste the bite of death.

The Envoy

After Sharon Monagle

Open the line of the poem   re-phrase the matter from
inside   the anterior wave of silence   remargin the
scorching hour   a woman   dust   covered & grief
burdened   something else   alive   or not   writes a
letter in dripping   sun   the writing is slow   blurs
does not   want to end   *through the window I saw no
sun   something   more sinister   towering column of smoke
rose behind   the hill   flaming bark fell from the sky   spot
fires rained down   embers   collected against the window
frame   flames gushed   forth   the skylight shattered   the
roof caved   in   the fire flared   flowed in furrows   crackling
as   unforeseen facts   roared & I   lurched
& burst   through the melting   flyscreen   burning tree roots
airborne   embers   something else   alive   or not   called
my name*   a woman   crust   coated & grief   struck
lover gone   lexicon shrunk to zilch   shivers & heaves
cracks & curses   in the scorching hour   legs curled
on   black   cinders   carpet.

Child's Play

Her hair is done up in funny macaroon buns on her ears, her eyes full, her mouth greedy. My little sister makes up my doll with Textas. Sapphire for the eyes, jet black for the eyebrows, fuchsia for the cheeks. She paints the lips vermillion, the nails, the navel, so that it's prettier. Then decides it's all wrong, scolds the doll, lectures her. Spanks her. Takes her in her arms, comforts her. Whispers burning words into her ear, rocks her gently. Sighs. She licks her fingers wet with saliva to remove some make-up, tilts her face towards me. And startles herself in my gaze. Let's play bride, she says. Doesn't wait for an answer, sticks glassy-eyed Leda in my hands. Together, we'll take turns to be the bride, with vaporous veil, and long train, lace gloves, nosegay of peonies, tiny sapphire satin pillow, gold rings… And all the dolls we'll sit in rows for the ceremony.

Between us, eye to eye, we learn and rehearse the butterfly kiss. Oooh, how that tickles!

Homo Ludens

Whiff of perfume. When I lie down on the couch my dreams slip away. The analyst is a pink lilac tree with fleshy nipples. A honeysuckle abuzz with bees. A wattle showering pollen. A cherry tree puffing under the weight of plump redness. I have much to do today, he says. But I love you. Speak, my love. *Little books sprout from our lips like flowers in a surrealist painting.* A bird crashes into the window and drops on the back veranda, wings spread out, beak wide open. I cup my palms over its ribcage. Feel its heart throb. I touch the analyst's hand. It's warm. The two of us, he says. Sunday. My father picks his teeth. Long yellow rabbit teeth. Yuck! *Hmm*, interrupts the analyst. I watch his ears. They quiver with each movement of his jaw. Large, fleshy ears stuck to his skull. Curly. Lots of creases and grooves. Furry and hollow in the middle. Furry tunnels, I mean funnels. My silent words pour in there. Cascade. Fall flat like giraffe words. My father's ears are deaf to my calls. Two massive doors with a locked safety screen each, a keyhole, peephole, bell and knocker. But no mailbox.

Anamnesis

The air shakes. Silver leafed emu bushes and climbing roses sway like a million ribbons in the breeze. Moonflowers close their fragrant white blooms. Acrid fumes sink into the pith of my lungs. Skeins of clouds unravel, dip in the deep, dissolve. There is no sun. No moon. Silence splinters and glows beyond the slowly fracturing sky. The horizon line is already underwater. A cormorant dives where oil slicks ripple on the water's grey surface seemingly drowning in its own weight. In the surf dark shadows glide and tumble, splash and paddle, glide and tumble. The wind picks up, vaporising the haze. Sand pecks at my skin. On the shore an army of women swathed in black and stooped dig out pipis and drop them in buckets. I paint them red. Sucking tide. Pong of rotting seal; maggots bloom from the open wound. Parenthesis of breath. There is no certainty that propagation will flourish on these planetary remains. I want to call the children out in the swell. No voice. I close my eyes. Wish myself back in time. Moonflowers open their fragrant blooms. Silver leafed emu bushes and climbing roses sway like a million ribbons in the breeze. The air unshakes.

Ξένος in the Sky

We came out of shelter full of glee, determined to occupy the band between infrared and radio waves so as not to be absorbed by interstellar dust. You gave me a submillimeter telescope to explore the regions of star formation and galactic nuclei. You had no idea I was making travel plans. The dog gone, you'd embraced Xanax and I, well, let's call sie Xenos. I spent all of my super on a stratospheric balloon with an über universe positioning system. I trained in the Himalayas. Taught myself Hungarian in case I encounter angels as I rise. Though you may not have noticed, my skin is now Big Bang proof. I'll see you in a couple of light years on the cusp of Teixidor. Meanwhile would you take care of my Chinese watercolours, African amulets, Russian dolls and French cameos? I bequeath to you my x-ray telescope for old times' sake. I left instructions on how to create an image of celestial bodies should you wish to explore the erotic possibilities of the spheres beyond the reach of intimate extimate gnosis.

PS: The freezer is stacked with chops for you to poise on my avatar's shoulder, Dalí-style.

Either / Or

Fear and trembling. My son's taken up knitting, so we drive to SPOTLIGHT for more wool. I'd hoped for a gratifying mother-son experience but the man of the house, being on permanent hols, is behind the wheel. I stitch my lips tight, metaphorically. We park. Dodge hailstones. Enter the shopping centre's arena. Show our immunisation certificates at the store's entrance. Head for CRAFT. I know the aisle like the back of my hand: here is the Classique premium acrylic yarn; there is the pure Australian wool made in China—either ply or entwine. The man knows ALL about yarn—either flammable or not. I cover my ears. Imagine I'm a cat perched on my grandmother's shoulder—definitely black. He's been done, and is therefore much larger than your customary feline: a small panther. The cat's name is Either / Or. A surge of heat. Something like the rush of air in a spot fire. Either I / Or the cat is being sucked down sticky shelves of incommunicado memories. Sinks into the floor, bound for the lowest display. Pounces. Slouches towards thick woolly chenille skeins. Long red claws prod, poke, unravel the four seasons yarn. Either crochet or cut. Excuse me, says the shop assistant. Eyes look up, Either / Or not after a pretext: Sorry, you must be looking for the wrong person.

Rhythm 0

After Louise Bourgeois

Everywhere, fragmented figures. Dismembered bodies. Here, four decapitated heads hung upside down from a dainty hook. All bandaged. She, the mother, tongue tied pink in white gauze criss-cross stitched black. Her babies, black currant and zipped. Slits for eyes, all. They do not see the sculptural space of their own staging. Do not know geometry's lexicon speaks fear's paralysing power. They just hang, contemporaneous.

To unravel a torment you must begin somewhere: Cut, rip, reconstruct, tear, repair; assemble, sew, darn, stuff, dye. All that pain, loss, betrayal. Unpicked.

Id prickles. A sweat breaks out on my skin. Jaws clench. Eyes fog. I send my gaze back from this unseeing lot to the unborn non sequiturs. Stripped naked, like soluble fish.

Inertia Carousel

Even what we can't, I do. What doesn't exist, I do. I dive in nothing. Swim long. Deep. Run together. I'm in free fall. Drown. A thousand times, I drown. The light! Such beauty I forget! Everything doesn't exist yet. I lick what doesn't exist. It tastes of stardust, air & fire. The Earth is sparkle & cerulean & lapis lazuli & mammoth & alive. Memories not mine behind eyelids. Hunting grounds. Teeth. Jaws & bones. Will-o'-the-wisps. Life rises behind pupils. Long breath. Everything lives, stops together & lives. My hands in the broken neck of matter glitter. Me? Ready for change. Phenomenal: spinning storm, plummeting sky. Protuberance of moons, mad passion of stones, black holes. A phenomenon beyond 41.3874° N, 2.1686° E, 2 PM. In the other world of what hasn't happened yet & plays out its own feverish symmetry I am sequential light. I see in the dark billions of miles away. Up to the stars where the Earth was Before. I soar to where things will be After. I know what I don't know. Hear what is not there. Touch its contours. Feel its pulse. Play the part.

Prosopagnosia

They call you Alice the chalice. You drink their faces like your own. You are porous. A vessel of diversion, a portmanteau artifact, a matryoshka doll, an infinite regression.

At the confluence of dreams, death and poetry:

Alices with // in Alices with // out Alices —

So many Elsas.

mise en abyme

      id is no longer   even

        a shape   e…merging

on calm black waters filled with sleeping stars…

You step into the river with rock hard dreams tied to your feet.

Aquatic

Gargling blood long rusted, you peel off the hull of the boat. Fly away on Zephyr's head in search of safer waters. In Crete you watch Icarus fall into Breughel's Aegean. You're not surprised to spot no Minotaur since History has it ensconced in the New World. You briefly find yourself in Lesbos, but decide its coast is too rugged. The wind complains. Mount Olympus is deserted, though there are rumours Melpomene, the only muse alive, is plotting The Deluge and drafting The Apocalypse. Hovering above the Thessaloniki Olympic pool you come upon a squadron of mermaids forming a rotating circle that creates whirling ripples on the water's surface. They break out swimming, perfectly synchronised. These are no mermaids, mind you, but long-limbed Gaia maids with beaming stage faces who perform flamingos and cranes, barracudas and knights, boosts and propeller skulls. What strength, skill, athleticism, timing and grace. What perfect balletting legs. What exquisite silence. You wish you'd seen the drone hovering above your ravished self. Now you're nothing save a split hair *twytwirling* in vacant air.

Εσπερινός

i.

All *asounder*. Nothing. We share an unpractised language, you and I. Something we thought we'd discarded with our younger selves when we'd cast words aside at night, picking them up next morning and tiring them out on foreign roads until dusk. We'd part, boxing our desires with attempts at forgetting our guilty pleasures. But words can't be boxed. They percolate through paper like espressos through paper cups, burning eager fingers, lips, tongues. They drive you to distraction, for they have the power of absenting themselves. I follow them now along creeks, rivers, shores, my body listening to the wind, skin suddenly alive, like phosphorus coming alight in air.

ii.

All *asounder*. Nothing. Thrustle rustling out to trick memory at the exact point where a plastic bag comes out of the mouth of a platypus. I see loss drown desire and love surge in a plume of rust. This is the time you say inside my head in my own tongue: *Rien*. Nothing. But a handful of gum leaves on the surface of the creek, rushing. They twirl, the leaves, disappear, swathed in dappled darkness. I'm a bubble bursting. Sheer effervescence, sigh, scent. Pepper, wattle, sunshine. Dragonfly wings pulsing in blue chill. High sweet E. Evanescence.

On the Heels of Fun

She hates kinder   checked paper   red stripe running from top to bottom   for the left margin   the red line has no twin on the page   annoys her like anything she colours inside the squares   changes hue with each   sticks out her tongue   finds the art of frieze and symmetry   though she doesn't know that yet   oh how much she misses her sister   can't wait for recess   she want to jump out the closed window……a pencil in each hand she alternates colouring   plays in a duet   she's a conductor   sometimes   she flies beyond her baton nooo   crosses the space   brims with anger   out of words   out of body   it spills out   she overflows and it overflows   her   this thing   so keen is she to fill the corner of her destiny   sorry   drawing   she doesn't see her arm leaning on the bottom of the folded page   a crease   she tries to smooth it out   it won't be a pretty drawing   who cares   she doesn't want to give it away nothing she makes is to give away   nothing will ever be pretty enough and she hates miss H   with her dirty eraser she starts to rub things out   it is so much more   *funfun.*

Fear of Birds

At the Monastero di San Giosefo del Ponte all'Oca birds carved into the vault spiralled downward around the columns, swooped and tangled your hair, auguring the sense of an ending already orbiting your world spectroscopically like a dead star.

Were you to come back from this Hitchcock parody, I would pull down the blinds, still the glassy gaze that took your breath. I would pluck out the mirror's black eyes.

I'm frightened of birds in spring when they light up the day with song. So, relentlessly, I paint birds of paradise in shades of cerulean through the enduring gold of violet remains when the air rustles its silvery white web, or hurtles its broken cockleshell dreams. They claw at death.

Swell

Hard as it is to imagine the Aegean casting off Orfeo's bones now silver water trailing in the Milky Way, his *piroga* song beading mother of pearl, you ask what is time, here where the sea, relentless mouth fights for breath, shade, light, feeds on night plumes tangled in a mullioned sky of sheer absence and sucks at Bass Strait's maelstrom of swirling white, here where fine-grained limestone slopes foam-crowned and crumbling, wash into blowholes as twilight seeps through furrowed rock wall awnings streaked with moonshine, here with its howling onshore gale swathed in the roar of the booming surf with its odour of kelp, salt hops, tea tree and rumours hovering in angel hair, or is it perhaps the mist, here curling where Eurydice's voice will all of a sudden break through the fractal arpeggios of sandpipers and cormorants pinking the shimmering breath of the sea as the sun sweeps its golden wave, here across time and distance and absence with salt spray whipping the red green cliff and the hooked beak of a rock eagle at the point where your face turns to stone, bone, silver, water, black moon.

Wabi-Sabi

Light falls in shafts. The crust of the earth loosens beneath your feet. You reach for the outline of your dissipating body

All around, no flowers in bloom
       Nor maple leaves in glare,
             A solitary fisherman's hut alone
                   On the twilight shore
                       Of this autumn eve

Ribbed hollowed out clay. Brittle to the touch. The feeling is full   empty. Duck feather breath weathering sun   wind rain   snow

Refracting shadows discolour
        tarnish
              warp
                      shrivel
                            crack
                                rust

Winter is floating lava. Black liquid smoke smoulders. Light peels off.

Flâneuses

It's November, or June. Today. Her name is Prose or Rose. Avid. And I, emptying. Already empty. *Vide.* How words climb back time across tongues, giving way to what can only be encountered step by step. Beat by beat.

Prose, or Rose, or you, voiceless; a thousand names for woman in a single glance, a thousand names encased in black, stir what's lost in silence. Names drift through the rose of dawn toward the Point Sublime and its ribbon of emerald water. Searing flash of light. Then day will break upon the worn words of constellations, flowers, rock formations and all will come alive in the indifferent sparkling of millenarian air proclaiming a slain name.

On the banks of the river Verdon streaming in light, we will pursue our journey, exploring extimate territories, tracking details of existences and places all the better to reveal the mysteries that merge through a shared desire to bury Eurydice's improbable destiny. We will turn stones over in the humming sunshine. Dig underneath rocks where snakes slip in sleep. Where mineral silence gives way to speech. Where the full size of the valley with its glimmering folds leads through twining tracks towards Voix.

Skin to Skin

She sits at the table, bathed in sunlight. Fiddles with play dough. Nibbles it with her nails, presses the dough with her hands. Prods and gropes like she can't see, shapes a body. You can't mix the colours, it's horrible, impossible to unmix. Bit by bit she feels a warmth that goes from her hand to the dough, from the dough to her hand, from flesh to flesh, skin to fingertip. Who will create the other? She would like to try first like she's a goddess. But doesn't dare. She flattens the dough with the palm of her hand, then stabs it again and again with a pen cap. She runs her fingers over the new form and feels its round, regular marks printed in relief. She tries it on her thigh. Her skin can't remember. She bites her lip. Her body calls for a lullaby: *Rock a bye 'be, on the table top / When my breath blows you will rock.* She pushes the tip of her tongue through the gap that was two front teeth. Red is her palette.

Punctum

Everyone as punctuation: you be an ellipsis signalling the omission from speech or writing of words that are unspeakable or superfluous. I take a tilde: the creased skin on my brow in the coming to writing. A gnashing of teeth. The hidden hook on my phone that purloins passwords. *La Reina de España*—from the Latin *Hispānia*, itself possibly derived from the Punic אִי שָׁפָן Say [esˈpaɲa]. You are at the Reales Alcázares de Sevilla. Go through the Puerta del León... Rush of guitar chords, castanets. Wailing. *Crescendo. Clap a clap clap. Clap clap. Click a clomp click. Clap clap clap. Clap clap.* Flourish. The flamenco dancer explodes into question marks. Night shatters into sparks. I aspire to the condition of umlaut: sharp, minimalist, pure calligraphic sign. The punctum that pricks me twice. The sign of cognitive dissonance in second life. Meet me there.

Fair Game

He's into sports. Beach and balls. We're in the same softball team. He invites me to his place, a house among trees that are stretched necks. It's autumn. Leaves turn copper, crunch underfoot into exuviae. At the confluence of numbness and forgetfulness, he takes me up to his room. We smoke fags at the window, rest our elbows on the windowsill. Where's your… Hush your mouth, he says. Our eyelids droop. We snort junk. Tie our heads with gossamer masks out of Magritte's 'The Lovers,' Sun unsung, the sky darkens with De Chirico clouds. We creep to a tan opening at the back of the room. Movement, the shape of a spectre staggering towards me. Mother, I say. Thank God you're here. She leads me to the opening. We're all here, she says. I notice the labyrinthine corridor has closed doors on either side. They're inside, she cackles. Everyone is. At the end of the room facing the passageway, a pair of eye-shaped windows clap shut. Waters begin to rise.

Reliquary

For Elizabeth Colbert

i.

Hand, blood orange broken into segments. Skin, russet crust. Fingernails unmooned and chipped. Palm, sand paper roughing out life and love lines. Open wounds leak, soak, seal. Scars itch, sting, burn away. Rain clings to the foot of the clouds.

ii.

You overlay three sheets of Washi paper. Trap grass, threads, lace between layers. Crooked fingers thread through cotton. You sew, scratch, stitch. With a quill, you trace curlicues of ink over a wash of crimson watercolour, swob of umber, smatter of gold dust. Thumb the dust. Rub. Shadows and fragments of bodies emerge. Then you stab grief with letters that dart, hook, nail like so many anchoring points on the edge of some catastrophe.

iii.

You suspend 'Blue like an Orange,' needle, thread, quill, inkpot with each watercolour vial and brush from the ceiling by a downpour of fine wires. Place a lightbulb at the centre of your composition so it catches fire.

iv.

Nothing more shows but marks, erasures and the fragile membrane stretched over the body of the world. A faint rainbow across the sky.

v.

The rising caws of crows. Your parchment hand cups all that remains. Is to come.

Schadenfreude

*To the tooposie hemtleposset – I like latchcomes
to rum at the sclorbets, don't you?*

Huff and puff of smoke from the fire, an empty glass of Captain Morgan, unsteady at midnight, ready to count the hours till break of day. Water everywhere. If you put words to paper in this weather, they'd scurry down the margins and away out of the house where streets are creeks swelling like the bellies of dead cows among posies of scarlet runners and *hemtlepossets*. All so not ready. The dog keens in his sleep. You speak to your other self, VoLTE voice aquiver. Canine tongue laps at your hand. *Lick. Lick Lick.* Blue lights blink outside the window. You rein in your galloping pulse. Lope down the corridor. Open the door. Freeze. A thousand green eyes inside walloping faces glare at you. The dog yelps. Grimacing humans gloat.

Gravity

Once upon a time the world was round and you could go on it around and around until she shot through like a Blakean thunderclap with all the forthrightness of childhood. She stood at the bay window. Said in a high, off-pitch voice: look at the moon. It bled and now shadows swallow it black. Her *nom de plume* was Gravity. Hurled me into the present.

Gravity is all Styrofoam. The skin on her whole body is lined from time's hot fibre. It squeals when I brush past her. She is the mite in Léger's eye, the carcinoma at the back of his retina. The pressed nothing on the canvas. She airs the studio. Voids narcissism. Erases equations.

She is the missing mass that neither creates electromagnetic radiation nor absorbs or scatters light from her surrounds. Some might say she is non-baryonic. Possibly non-Blakean. Definitely non-Byronic. Totally no ordinary matter.

Though on (¿) call I suggest she change her *nom de plume*.

Presence Follows Function

The knighted man arrives on his *pur sang arabe* like a breeze in a dark alley. He dismounts. I doff my *chapel-de-fer*. Check my *bevor*, just in case. But he has no lance. He ties up his horse. Twirls around on his exquisitely pointed sollerets. Legs jelly, I muster courage from the reflection of the free-flowing form and spiral fluting of my broad-rimmed *chapel-de-fer* reflected in moonlight. The beautiful man regards me through his visor, mere slit in his sleek Milanese helmet. I scrutinise the flexible shell that espouses his entire body without, it seems, impeding mobility. The neck guards are winglets. No cuirie on the plastron. The tace and tacet are all streamlined, as are the cuish and greave: no knee cop to speak of. Oh, lo and behold: the codpiece is made of supple chainmail. We hook arms, amble down the alley. Bump into Saints Christopher, Eustace and Erasmus. Round the corner, we greet Madonna and Dalí seated at a dingy table outside a restaurant opposite the Pompidou. 'Be my guest', says Dalí, twirling his moustache, 'lobster obliges.' We sit down, wondering what these two supremely beautiful people might say about functional beauty. Madonna hoots. Orders another bottle of Sancerre. Tymbals!

Breathless

After Jean-Luc Godard

... ... begins on a runway as thin as a Beckett plot with cocky Michel puffing away if you don't like the sea or the mountains or the big city go fuck yourself. A gawk in the rear vision mirror. Jibe at the camera. *La la la*...A gun. *Pan!* The cop is dead. Who cares? Cocky wants to bolt to Rome with cool Patricia. Michel is Humphrey Bogart with a grim twinkle in his eyes. He's muscle-bound. An actor bordering on caricature. He'd rather be a jaguar on the prowl. Life is a bluff. Keep moving. Posh Paris swirls around the pair. You hang out with them : L'Arc de Triomphe, les Champs Elysées, Place de la Concorde postcard-like night-lit. Clichés. The film cuts to Patricia's translucent face. She says: I've been staring at you for the past ten minutes and I can't see anything but a mask. A police manhunt closes in on us. *We are dead men on leave.*

Centaurs

After Utte Isolotto

We start where the wall breaks and the river bursts its banks past La Rosette. We could call the *sapeurs-pompiers*, but walk the earth instead, half swan, half goose. When clothes no longer fit around our changing bodies, we drape horse skins around our torsos. We grow hair long and thick on our lengthening legs. Come spring the equine skins come loose. We shed. Hooves push through where once were feet. We teeter on their narrowness. The hair on our horse parts grows back dappled grey and shiny. We push on through hills and valleys. In the mountains we reach a deserted farmhouse with a ham still hanging from a hook in the kitchen. The shed is stacked with hay. You cluck your tongue when you discover eggs preserved in a vat of fat at the back. I clap eyes on mounds of potatoes, swedes and turnips. Sniff water: a well in the yard. I hoist the bucket. Taste the water. It's good. We quench our thirst. After love, you say: what if we are creating a species that means trouble? I chortle, relieved you haven't lost the power of speech.

We never thought we'd end it there, but parturition changed everything. The creature came. You hanged yourself. I can't hold breath.

The Doors

i.

The house rocks like a boat tugging at its moorings. Inner weather, gusty. We're playing dead fish. Mike Parr's 'Head on a Plate' regards me. I stare back. I'm gone with the wind, gills and fins fluttering. Disappear the golden orb spinning its silk threads in cirrhus clouds branching against the sky. Unstick myself from the idea of arachnophobia and away from the viscid spiral of sticky thread joining windowpane to Parr's etching. The head is distorted. I blink off the shadowed eye sockets. Squint. With a slight adjustment of perspective, I catch sight of an anamorphic skull: *punKtime*. Death brushes past. We are *The Ambassadors* now, waiting for Godot. Maestro strides in through the lounge's butter doors. Opens the baby grand's lid. Fingers scurry on the keyboard. Hammers hammer strings. The floorboards shake. Walls are reefs. I'm a jellyfish. Starfish. Rock fish. A rolling stone that doesn't know what it sways. 'God, ready?' Nose aloft, the dog holds my gaze. 'Roll. Left. Right. Left. Right. Turn and toss.' Fur and silk ripple. Passage of blazing light as backdrop. Melting butter. We are The Doors now. Heterodogsia, unsinging the dance. *Körperbild. People are Strange*, my dog. Rock!

ii.

At night, when silence trembles with echoes and moonshine bobs on the floorboards casting shards of shadows on the walls, we leave them open to the dark, the doors. To terrorise the Architect who looks down upon this phantom world *in ille tempore*. Because all life holds its own destruction and God is nothing but the arbitrary distinction between heaven and earth, left and right, margin and *immargination*. Cut, not suture. Kinetic poesis. No beginning, but rhythm, repetition, spacing, caesura: difference from self. Dog centre. Repercussion, resonance, reverberation, resounding, revenance, reflection, return from within difference. Humans or otherwise, we are constituted by rhythm. This caesura sentence which gathers and segments and which means that every single thing can be danced like a prose poem unleashing the rules of lexis, grammar, syntax. In ruffle reef light, fur and silk ripple and brush. *Time is paradoxical… it folds or twists; it is as various as the dance of flames in a brazier, here interrupted, there vertical, mobile and unexpected.* Because we are truly fickle matter existing. Already exiting. Rocking the boat to the breath of time.

Contexts

In art as in life, the 'volte face', when someone turns around to confront someone else, is understood as being a moment of truth and a gesture of recognition that implies the acknowledgment of the other and the assertion of the self. The volte face is the experience of making sense of the senseless such as Greek letters masquerading as mathematical symbols. It functions as a punctuation mark. It creates a moment of tension and high expectation that generates an affect. More often than not, this affect is the anguish generated by the tacit question 'what do you want from me'?

In this collection I seek to create this moment of truth, this gesture of recognition, this event of making sense of the senseless by using 'extraliterary' connotations sourced from other disciplines, including psychoanalysis and philosophy to enhance the ludic dimension of the text. The interplay of images functions in a similar fashion. There are, therefore, no 'sections' in this work, only kinetic and kaleidoscopic gestures, and affects other than anguish.

The epigraphs are from James Joyce's *Finnegans Wake*. (Faber, 1966, p. 12) and Le Corbusier's *Towards a New Architecture* (CPSIA, n.d., p. 3).

Roland Barthes coins the term 'extraliterary' in *Camera Lucida: Reflections on Photography*. (trans. Richard Howard, Hill & Wang 1981, p. 169).

Notes to Poems

p.1 Borges and I refers to one of Jorge Luis Borges' famous parables published in the collection *Labyrinths*. (Penguin, 1970, pp. 282-83).

p.4 The Sound of Air responds ekphrastically to Jean-Michel Folon's 'Rain' sculpture. (*'Pluie'*, 1996, Ferme du Château de la Hulpe, Belgium).

p.6 The italicised phrase in **The Entombment** is sourced from Coleridge's 'Kubla Khan.' (*The Penguin Book of English Verse*. John Hayward (ed.), Penguin, p. 256).

p.7 Anaphora takes its title from Elizabeth Bishop's poem of the same name. The opening echoes Bishop's first two lines. (*Poems*. Ferrar, Strauss and Giroux, 2011, p. 52).

p.9 The Lord of the Rats and Eke of Mice takes its title from Goethe's *Faust*, Chapter III.

The line 'Move upward, working out the beast' is from Tennyson's 'In Memoriam,' CXVIII. *Poems of Tennyson*. Henry Frowde (ed.), Oxford UP, 1904, p. 433).

p.11 Five Bells takes its title from Kenneth Slessor's famous elegy. (*Poems*, Angus and Robertson, 1972, pp. 121-24). Like Slessor's poem, it engages with the legend of Joe Lynch from the writing persona's subjective experience, within a time span of three minutes.

p.14 Archives of the Future is an ekphrastic response to Oscar Dominguez's 1938 oil painting *Lembranca do Futuro*. (Tenerife Espacio de las Artes, Spain).

There is an obvious allusion to W. B. Yeats's 'The Second Coming' in lines 1-2 to convey a sense of anxiety about the future. (*Selected Poetry*, Pan Books, 1974, p. 99).

p.19 Ekphrastic Still: '*l'amur*' is a Lacanian pun melding 'amour' / 'love' and 'mur' / 'wall.' The capitalisation of the term in the piece is an ironic spin on Lacan's own term to suggest that *l'amur* is on the side of the Symbolic.

p.23 How It Is: the phrase 'Sitting figure in decomposition' alludes to Dalí's 'Kneeling Figure in Decomposition.' (1950, The Salvador Dalí Museum, St Petersburg, Florida).

p.24 Champagne Supernova, Taché: 'The world's still spinning round, we don't know why' and part of the title are taken from Oasis's famous song 'Champagne Supernova.'

p.27 In writing **Head Study**, quotations from various sources came to mind:

> The line 'anger makes one clench one's teeth, terror and atrocious suffering make the mouth the organ of tearing cries' is from Georges Bataille's 'La bouche' (*Documents*, no 5, 1930, p. 300).

> Julia's words are from Julia Kristeva, 'Bataille, l'expérience et la pratique.' (*Bataille*, Philippe Sollers ed, Gallimard, 1973, p. 65).

> 'And squirting out a sharp death-gush of blood, / He strikes me with dark drizzle of murderous dew,' are Aeschylus' actual lines (*The Oresteia*, trans. R. Eagles, Faber, 1976, p. 50).

p.32 Magritte's Gravestone: the first part of this piece is lifted or manipulated from Suzi Gablik's *Magritte*. (Thames & Hudson, 1976, pp. 102-108). The second part is surreal conjecture.

p.34 A Haunting: Bernd Heinrich Wilhelm von Kleist (1777 -1811) was a German poet, dramatist, novelist, short story writer and journalist. He died by suicide together with a friend, Henriette Vogel, who was terminally ill.

p.35 Oblivion: Freud's words are direct quotations from his essay 'Childhood Memories and Screen Memories,' (*The Standard Edition of the Complete Psychological Works of Sigmund Freud*, vol. 6, 1901, Hogarth Press, 1960, p. 43).

p.36 Less Is a Bore: It is the American architect Robert Venturi who coined the phrase 'less is a bore.' This prose poem draws on a photograph of the house he designed for his mother.

p.38 Magpies: Hyères is a town in the South of France. Its name is homonymous with '*hier*,' meaning 'yesterday.'

p.41 Endgame with No Ending: The title of Jonathan Foer's *Tree of Codes* exhumes and manipulates *The Street of Crocodiles*, a book of stories by Bruno Schultz (Penguin, 2008). In fact, as Foer tells us in an afterword, *Tree of Codes* is 'a die-cut book by erasure' of Schultz' work. (Visual Editions, 2010, p. 138).

p.43 Bird Returning to its Nest takes its title from a painting by Georges Braque. (1959, Centre Pompidou, Paris, France).

The line 'A painter knows what to do by the tug of the brush' is from James Elkin's *What Painting Is*. (Routledge, 1999, p. 78).

p.45 Blood Lines: René Magritte seems to have been obsessed with memory. ('La mémoire,' 1948, Musée d'Ixelles, Brussels, Belgium).

p.47 Liquid Desire alludes to Salvador Dalí's 'Birth of Liquid Desires' (1931-32, Guggenheim Collection, New York). It was also the title of the 2009 retrospective of his work curated by the National Gallery of Victoria, Melbourne. All the artefacts mentioned in this piece are Dalí objects.

p.48 Evridiki is the Greek spelling of Eurydice

p.49 The Envoy takes its title from Jane Hirschfield's poem of the same name. (https://www.poetryfoundation.org/poems/47097/the-envoy). It contains a number of words from that poem as well as from Ted Hughes's 'The Thought Fox.' (https://poetryarchive.org/poem/thought-fox/).

The piece responds ekphrastically to Sharon Monagle's artwork *Alchemy*, 2018, *Poetry of Encounter*, eds. Anne M Carson, Rose Lucas, Renee Pettitt-Schipp (Liquid Amber Press, 2022)

p.51 Homo Ludens appropriates, with the author's permission, a line from Michael Farrell's *Family Trees*. (Giramondo, 2020, p. 88).

p.55 Rhythm 0 responds to Louise Bourgeois' *Cinq 2007*. The italicised words are taken from her portfolio of nine letterpress and lithograph diptychs 'What is the Shape of this Problem,'(1990, Art Gallery of South Australia).

p.57 Prosopagnosia, or face-blindness, cites Rimbaud's 'Ophélie,' (*Arthur Rimbaud: Complete Works*, Wyatt Mason trans, Modern Library, 2003, p. 77).

p.59 Εσπερινός: Esperinos: an evening song or prayer which evokes the morning star. I use Greek characters in the title to intimate the disjunction that language introduces in human relationships.

p.61 Fear of Birds takes its title from Margaret Atwood's poem of the same name. (*Dearly*, Vintage, 2020 p. 75).

p.62 Swell: In 2020, Italo Lanfrendini commissioned a poem that sings and breathes the sea to accompany his *Piroga* project. I sent 'Swell' / 'Houle' with an Italian translation. Poems in numerous languages were displayed around the boat after the 2021 lockdown, then launched to sea. 'Piroga' and 'Orfeo' are traces of the project.

p.63 In **Wabi-Sabi** the italicised lines are taken from a poem by Fujiwara no Teika, trans. Toshihiko and Toyo Izutsu, in Leonard Koren's *Wabi-Sabi for Artists, Designers, Poets & Philosophers*. (Imperfect Publishing, 2008, p. 55).

p.64 The French for voice in **Flâneuses**, '*voix*,' is a parapraxis. The real name of the town alluded to in the piece is Volx.

p.66 Punctum takes literally Barthes' notion of punctum. (*Camera Lucida*, Richard Howard trans, Hill & Wang, 1981, p. 47).

p.70 Schadenfreude cites *Finnegans Wake* (Op. Cit., p. 13).

p.71 The phrase 'Once upon a time the world was round and you could go on it around and around' in **Gravity** opens Gertrude Stein's *The World is Round*. (Harper Design, 2013, p. 1).

p.73 Breathless quotes Eugen Leviné's last words 'We are dead men on leave.' (https://www.marxists.org/subject/germany-1918-23/levine/last-words.htm)

p.74 Centaurs responds to *We Walked the Earth*, an installation by Utte Isoloto housed at the Danish Pavilion, 59th Venice Biennale, 2022.

p.75 The Doors references the album *Strange Days* by The Doors, 1967. The italicised lines are from Roland Barthes's *Camera Lucida*, op. cit.

Acknowledgements

I acknowledge the Wurundjeri Woi Wurrung of the Kulin Nation, Traditional Owners of the land on which these poems were written. I pay my respects to First Nations Elders past and present.

Grateful acknowledgement is made to the editors of the following, in which some of these poems, or versions of them, originally appeared: *Axon*; *Aesthetica Creative Award 2022*; *Dancing Towards Architecture* (eds. Cassandra Atherton and Oz Hardwick), *Décision*; *Live Encounters*, *Not Very Quiet*; *Play: An Anthology of the Joanne Burns Microlit Award 2023* (ed. Cassandra Atherton); *Poetry of Encounter: The Liquid Amber Prize Anthology 2022* (eds. Anne M. Carson and Rose Lucas); *Rabbit*; *Remnants: An Anthology of the Joanne Burns Microlit Award 2024* (ed. Cassandra Atherton), *Shadows and Tall Trees*; *Speculate*; *Tiny Spoon*; *Travel: An Anthology of the Joanne Burns Microlit Award 2022* (ed. Cassandra Atherton); *Western Humanities Review*.

Special thanks to The ScAN/AAWP Neuroscience and Creative Writing Collaboration Project for commissioning work in response to three digital images of the human brain, 2019-23. Also, huge thanks to the community of writers and readers from the Prose Poetry Project at IPSI, and to Catherine Clover for inviting me to participate in 'Wild Energies: Live Materials', a symposium held at the Creative Research into Sound Arts Practice department at the University of Arts, London, 2022.

About the Author

Dominique Hecq was born in the French-speaking part of Belgium. She now lives on unceded Wurundjeri land in Melbourne, Australia. Hecq writes in English and French. Her creative works comprise a novel, six collections of short stories and fifteen books and chapbooks of poetry. Her latest publications include *After Cage* (2nd ed., 2022, Liquid Amber Press), *Endgame with No Ending* (2023, SurVision) and a bilingual poetry sequence titled *Pistes de rêve / Songlines,* with photographs by Natia Zvhania (Transignum, 2024).

Among other honours such as The Melbourne Fringe Festival Award for Outstanding Writing and Spoken Word Performance, The Woorilla Prize for Fiction, The New England Review Prize for Poetry, The Martha Richardson Medal for Poetry, and the inaugural AALITRA Prize for Literary Translation (Spanish to English), Dominique Hecq is a recipient of the International Best Poets Prize administered by the International Poetry Translation and Research Centre in conjunction with the International Academy of Arts and Letters and, more recently, the James Tate Poetry Prize.